W9-CBR-136

THE MONARCHS
ARE MISSING
A Butterfly Mystery

Rebecca E. Hirsch

Millbrook Press/Minneapolis

To my father, Herm Stange, lover of wild things

Title page: This close-up of a monarch's wing shows the thousands of tiny scales that give the wings their color.

Text copyright © 2018 by Rebecca E. Hirsch

All rights reserved. International copyright secured. No part of this book may be reproduced, stored in a retrieval system, or transmitted in any form or by any means—electronic, mechanical, photocopying, recording, or otherwise—without the prior written permission of Lerner Publishing Group, Inc., except for the inclusion of brief quotations in an acknowledged review.

Millbrook Press
A division of Lerner Publishing Group, Inc.
241 First Avenue North
Minneapolis, MN 55401 USA

For reading levels and more information, look up this title at www.lernerbooks.com.

Main body text set in Adrianna 12/20.
Typeface provided by Chank.

Library of Congress Cataloging-in-Publication Data

Names: Hirsch, Rebecca E.
Title: The monarchs are missing : a butterfly mystery / by Rebecca E. Hirsch.
Description: Minneapolis : Millbrook Press, [2018] | Audience: Age 8–12. | Audience: Grade 4 to 6. | Includes bibliographical references and index. | Identifiers: LCCN 2017010743 (print) | LCCN 2017011789 (ebook) | ISBN 9781512498660 (eb pdf) | ISBN 9781512452501 (lb : alk. paper)
Subjects: LCSH: Monarch butterfly—Juvenile literature. | Monarch butterfly— Losses—Juvenile literature. | Monarch butterfly—Migration—Juvenile literature. | Monarch butterfly—Conservation—Juvenile literature. | Butterflies—Losses— Juvenile literature. | Butterflies—Conservation—Juvenile literature.
Classification: LCC QL561.D3 (ebook) | LCC QL561.D3 H574 2018 (print) | DDC 595.78/9—dc23

LC record available at https://lccn.loc.gov/2017010743

Manufactured in the United States of America
1-42918-26515-8/31/2017

CONTENTS

Monarchs fuel their migration with nectar from fall wildflowers, such as the goldenrod in this Pennsylvania field.

INTRODUCTION
Bye-Bye Butterflies?

On a warm September afternoon, a monarch butterfly flies over a Pennsylvania field full of goldenrod. The monarch skims over the bright yellow flowers, fluttering south toward the distant trees.

Whoosh!

A net swings in from the side, and the monarch is caught. A hand wraps around the fabric at the top of the net. Now there is no escape. The hand belongs to Joe, who is twelve years old. He is going to let the butterfly go again, but first, he has a job to do. He pinches the orange-and-black wings closed through the soft fabric of the net. This does not hurt the insect. Then he reaches inside the net with his other hand and carefully pulls the monarch out.

By holding the net closed, Ellie (*top*) prevents this monarch from escaping. The tagged butterfly (*bottom*) takes a walk on Joe's arm before lifting off.

Joe's partner, twelve-year-old Ellie, comes up beside him with a clipboard. She writes down today's date, the location, and the butterfly's sex. This monarch has a single black dot on each hind wing, which means it's a male. Joe holds the wings closed as Ellie presses a tiny sticker firmly on one hind wing.

Now it is time for the captive's release. Joe places the monarch in his free hand. The butterfly walks along his arm, opens and closes its wings a few times, and lifts silently into the air. It catches a breeze and soars, wings open, across the field of goldenrod, over the trees, and out of sight.

This monarch is going on a mysterious journey. Millions of monarchs will join it, flying up to 3,000 miles (4,828 km) from across the eastern United

Male monarch butterflies (*left*) have thinner veins and scent pouches on the upper side of their hind wings, while females (*right*) have thicker veins and no scent pouches.

scent pouch

States and Canada, all the way to Mexico. The trip is quite a feat for a creature that flies on paper-thin wings and weighs about as much as a raisin. In fact, it is one of the world's great animal migrations.

But the monarchs are in danger. The number of monarchs reaching Mexico has been decreasing over the past twenty years. The winter of 2013–2014 marked the fewest monarchs ever recorded in Mexico. To protect these insects and their amazing migration, scientists must understand what is going wrong. They rely on citizen scientists—people like Joe and Ellie—to make observations and collect data in the field. Together, scientists and citizen scientists are trying to solve a mystery: Why are the monarchs disappearing?

The winter conditions that monarchs need to survive are found in just a handful of mountaintop forests in Mexico, like this one near Angangueo, Michoacán.

CHAPTER 1
The Mysterious Monarch Migration

The migration of monarch butterflies has long been a mystery for scientists. Until the 1970s, American and Canadian scientists didn't know where monarchs went every winter. They knew that the familiar backyard butterflies laid their eggs in fields of milkweed across North America every summer. They knew that the Rocky Mountains split the monarchs into two large populations. They knew that the western monarchs—those living west of the Rocky Mountains—migrated to a long stretch of the California coast, where they spent each winter clustered in groves of trees. As for the much larger population living east of the Rockies, scientists knew only that those monarchs flew south in the fall. But where did the monarchs' migration end?

At the same time, in a few mountain villages in central Mexico, residents were also puzzled. Every November, millions of black-and-orange *mariposas* poured through the villages on their way to the nearby forests. Their arrival coincided with Dia de los Muertos (Day of the Dead), a holiday to remember friends and family members who have died. Some people said the butterflies were the returning souls of departed loved ones.

Poet Homero Aridjis, who grew up in one of those villages, remembers the arrival of the butterflies. "When the sun was out, rivers of butterflies would stream through the streets in search of water," he wrote. Like others in the village, he didn't know where the butterflies had come from. He didn't know they had flown there from across the United States, as far away as Canada.

In 1935 Canadian scientist Fred Urquhart became determined to discover where the eastern monarchs were spending the winter. He knew he couldn't solve the mystery simply by following the monarchs, as butterflies are impossible to follow over land for very far. He thought about how ornithologists attach numbered metal bands around the legs of birds. The band allows an observer to report back each bird's location to scientists, who use that information to track its movements.

Urquhart realized he needed a way to mark an individual butterfly so it could be identified wherever it traveled. That way, if a monarch that had been tagged and released in Toronto was later recaptured in Texas, it would be a clue to the monarchs' winter destination.

He first tried marking monarchs with dyes, paints, and even radioactive material. He sprayed

Fred Urquhart persisted until he found a method of tagging butterflies that would work.

the butterflies with a spray gun or stamped a number on their wings, then released them. But no observers ever reported back to him the whereabouts of those marked butterflies. It dawned on him that the tag needed to carry instructions so observers would know what to do. So he turned to paper tags, each printed with a unique number and the words "Send to Zoology, University [of] Toronto, Canada." He tried gluing the tags onto the wings, but the glue stuck to his fingers and made it difficult to handle the butterflies.

Somewhere along the way, he began to enlist the help of his wife, Norah. Next, the Urquharts turned to stickers. But some stickers wouldn't adhere to the smooth wings. Other stickers washed off in the rain. Finally, the Urquharts tried a tag based on the price stickers used in grocery stores. They folded each sticky tag over a monarch's wing. It worked. The tags remained in place.

In 1952 the Urquharts invited members of the public to help them tag and release monarchs all across North America, and to keep their eyes open for tagged butterflies. An observer who found a tagged butterfly could mail either the tag or the tagged dead insect back to the Urquharts. By 1964 hundreds of volunteers had tagged about seventy thousand monarchs. Every time a tagged monarch was recovered, the Urquharts plotted its flight path on a map. A picture began to emerge. Monarchs that lived east of the Rocky Mountains always headed toward Mexico.

The Urquharts teamed up with a couple living in Mexico: Ken Brugger and Cathy Aguado. Together with their dog, Kola, the couple crisscrossed the countryside in their motor home, searching for monarchs. They eventually tracked the butterflies to a region of high volcanic mountains west of Mexico City.

On a cold day in January 1975, Brugger, Aguado, and a local helper were climbing the Cerro Pelon Mountain. Aguado was in the lead when she gazed up and saw oyamel (oy-EE-ah-mel) trees covered with millions of monarchs. "I see them, I see them!" she shouted. In the next few weeks, the couple found more monarch colonies, all high in the mountains in forests of oyamels, which are a kind of fir tree.

The Urquharts visited the following winter. "Masses of butterflies—everywhere!" Fred Urquhart later wrote. Millions upon millions of monarchs clustered in the trees. They covered the trunks. They clung to the branches, which bent low under their weight.

But were these the eastern monarchs, the same ones that flew in backyards and fields east of the Rocky Mountains? The answer came when a branch broke and hundreds of butterflies crashed to the ground. As Fred Urquhart leaned in for a closer look,

The August 1976, issue of *National Geographic*, with Cathy Aguado on the cover, announced to the world that the eastern monarch's winter home had been found.

he spotted a butterfly with a white tag folded over its wing. "I could not have been more excited if I had uncovered a buried treasure," he later wrote. By chance he'd found a monarch that had been tagged by two students and their teacher in Chaska, Minnesota, nearly 1,800 miles (2,900 km) away.

Fred Urquhart—with plenty of help—had solved the mystery at last. Eastern monarchs flew up to thousands of miles to spend winter in the mountains of central Mexico. Since that discovery, scientists have found about twelve overwintering sites in Mexico, all in high mountain forests full of oyamels.

THE AMAZING MIGRATORY RELAY

No one knows how or when the monarch migration began. But it may have started when the last ice age ended, about ten thousand years ago. During the last ice age, milkweed may have grown only in what is now Mexico and Central America. Milkweed is the monarch's host plant. Milkweed isn't a single plant species; it is rather a group of plants that includes over one hundred individual species. Female monarchs lay their eggs only on milkweed, and the caterpillars eat only this plant. So monarchs breed only in places where milkweed grows. When the last ice age ended, and the cold and glaciers retreated, milkweed may have gradually spread northward, and monarchs may have followed. But the monarch butterfly remained a tropical creature, unable to survive the severe northern winters. So every year as winter approached, monarchs left their summer fields of milkweed and flew south again. To this day, every spring and summer, monarchs travel north to their breeding grounds across the eastern United States and Canada. Every winter, they return to Mexico.

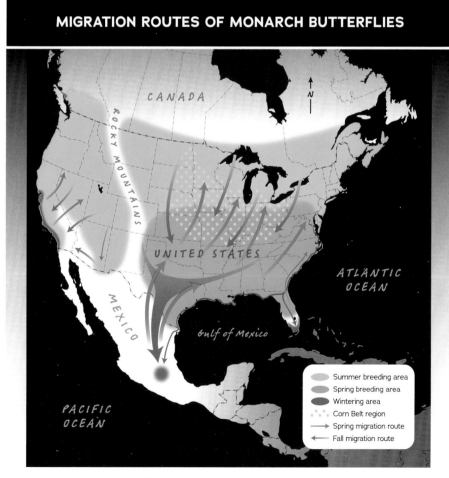

MIGRATION ROUTES OF MONARCH BUTTERFLIES

CANADA

ROCKY MOUNTAINS

UNITED STATES

MEXICO

ATLANTIC OCEAN

Gulf of Mexico

PACIFIC OCEAN

N

- Summer breeding area
- Spring breeding area
- Wintering area
- Corn Belt region
- → Spring migration route
- ← Fall migration route

This map shows migration routes of fall and spring migrations, both east and west of the Rocky Mountains.

Upon their arrival in Mexico, monarchs spend winter in a partially dormant state. Clustered together in dense colonies, they rest in the trees and live off fat they have stored in their abdomens. On warm days, masses of monarchs leave the trees to find water. The flapping of their wings rustles like a gentle rain. The butterflies drink from pools and streams and then quickly return to the safety of the trees. If the temperature were to drop even briefly—such as when the sun goes behind a cloud—they could be stranded on the ground. They are cold-blooded creatures and cannot fly when the temperature falls below 55°F (13°C). For a butterfly, the ground is dangerous. A monarch on the ground could get eaten by a mouse or other predator, or it could get wet and freeze to death. So the monarchs spend most of their time in the trees, where they're protected.

In spring the monarchs become active. Males pursue females, and they mate as they begin to fly north. The journey north resembles a relay race, with different generations completing different parts of the journey. The females from the oyamel forests lay their eggs on milkweed across northern Mexico, Texas, and other parts of the southern United States. Then the males and females from the forests die.

Monarch butterflies pack together for warmth in the winter sanctuaries. These monarchs are in the El Capulin colony in Macheros, Mexico.

As a caterpillar eats (*left*), milkweed poisons build up in its body. The stripes warn animals that the caterpillar is poisonous. Inside the chrysalis (*right*), the caterpillar's body parts are rearranging. It grows new antennae, compound eyes, and wings, while old body parts that are no longer needed break down.

But the migration north does not end there. In about a week, a caterpillar hatches from each egg. First, the caterpillar devours its eggshell, and after that, it eats milkweed leaves. Milkweed contains poisons, and most animals won't eat it. But the monarch caterpillar thrives on it. The caterpillar collects the poisons in its body, and so it too becomes poisonous to many predators. The poisons will remain in its body when it becomes a butterfly.

As the young caterpillar grows, it molts, or sheds its skin. In a few weeks the caterpillar sheds its skin one last time, emerging as a jade-green chrysalis decorated with gold dots. This stage is also called a pupa. Another week or two passes, then the skin of the chrysalis splits open. The adult monarch wiggles its legs through the widening crack and drags itself out. It hangs from the empty chrysalis skin and pumps fluid into its shriveled wings to expand them to full size. Within hours it is ready to fly.

LIFE CYCLE OF A MONARCH BUTTERFLY

egg
3–5 days

larva
11–18 days

egg to adult
22–37 days
at 72°F–82°F
(22°C–28°C)

chrysalis
8–14 days

adult

The adult butterfly has a long, tube-shaped mouth and eats only nectar, the sugary liquid found inside of flowers.

The offspring continue flying north. Along the way, they mate, and the females lay eggs on milkweed. Soon that generation of males and females dies, and their offspring continue the migration. By summer the monarchs have spread all the way into southern Canada, the far northern edge of where milkweed can grow. The monarchs will spread no farther.

Throughout the summer, monarchs breed wherever milkweed grows, and the population increases. Each female might lay seven hundred eggs over the course of her three- to four-week life span. But fewer than 5 percent of those eggs will reach adulthood. Diseases and parasites will infect and kill many offspring. Predators will kill more. The caterpillars do have some protection from predators through the milkweed poisons they eat. And although both the caterpillars and the butterflies display bright colors to warn predators that they are poisonous, this coloring protects them from only some birds and mammals. Spiders, ants, wasps, and some songbirds will still prey on the caterpillars. So a female monarch, by laying a large number of eggs, increases the chance that some of her offspring will survive. Fortunately, enough of her offspring do survive, and the monarch population grows and grows until late summer and early fall, when the last of the monarchs emerge from their chrysalises.

The final generation is different from the spring and summer butterflies. For them, the short, cool days of fall and the yellowing milkweed plants are a signal to migrate. These butterflies enter diapause, which means they don't mate or lay eggs. Instead, they feast hungrily on nectar and store fat for the journey ahead. The stored fat will help them live through the winter. The cool weather in the forest will also help them live longer, by slowing their metabolism. Unlike summer monarchs, which live for about a month, the migrating monarchs can live for as long as nine months, if they make it to Mexico.

When metamorphosis is complete, the chrysalis case splits and the adult butterfly emerges (*left*). Butterflies feed on nectar, which is about 90 percent water and 10 percent sugar. This monarch (*right*) is drinking nectar with its long, tube-shaped proboscis.

The fall migration begins slowly in mid-August. The northernmost monarchs are the first to go. They fly south on warm, clear days, using sunshine to warm their bodies. They save energy by rising on thermals (currents of warm, rising air) and then gliding on the wind with their wings open. They fuel up often, stopping to drink nectar from fall flowers, and most of them will actually gain weight on the trip. They must arrive fat and healthy to survive winter in the forest.

As the migration continues, more and more monarchs join the journey south. By the time the butterflies reach Texas, they are streaming across the sky.

The monarchs trickle into the Mexican forests starting in early November. No one knows how they know where to go, as they've never been to the oyamel forests before. The butterflies that arrive in the forests are the great-grandchildren and the great-great-grandchildren of those that left Mexico the year before.

THE MYSTERY OF THE MISSING MONARCHS

The fact that all eastern monarchs cluster on a few mountains gave researchers an opportunity to estimate the size of the entire eastern population. That isn't possible in the summer, when the eastern monarchs are spread across half a continent. It's not possible in the spring or fall either, when they are on the move. But in winter, all the eastern monarchs are concentrated in just a handful of spots. Estimating the size of the population would give scientists a way to keep track of how the eastern monarchs were doing from year to year.

But how could researchers count so many butterflies? It's impossible to count them one by one—there are simply too many. Instead, researchers measure the area of the colonies. Every year, no matter how many monarchs there are, the butterflies cluster together in the trees. In years with a lot of monarchs, the colonies cover a bigger area of forest. In years with fewer monarchs, they cover a smaller area.

To measure the size of a colony, researchers walk through the forest and first decide which trees have enough butterflies to count as part of the colony. Then they mark the trees at the edge of the colony and measure the distance between them. They repeat this at each of the twelve overwintering sites. From these measurements, they calculate the total area of all the colonies, which gives them a rough estimate of the size of the eastern monarch population.

So what did these yearly estimates reveal about the eastern monarchs? Researchers began taking measurements in 1993. The highest year on record came in 1997, when the colonies covered about 45 acres (18 ha), an area equal to about thirty-four football fields. Scientists aren't sure exactly how many butterflies that represented, but one estimate is that there were one billion monarchs in the colonies that winter.

But as researchers measured the colonies year after year, they noticed that the colonies were shrinking. By 2014 the colonies measured just 1.7 acres (0.7 ha), or less than one and a half football fields. That year there may have been only about thirty-five million monarchs in the colonies.

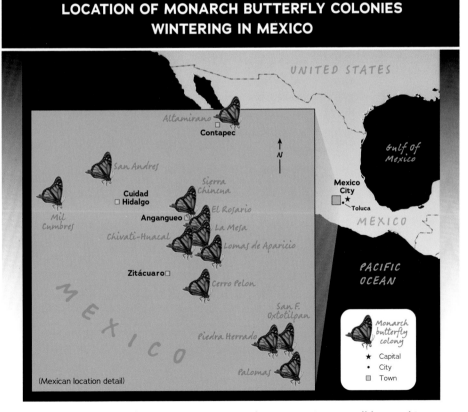

LOCATION OF MONARCH BUTTERFLY COLONIES WINTERING IN MEXICO

UNITED STATES

Altamirano
Contapec

San Andres

Sierra Chincua

Cuidad Hidalgo

El Rosario

Mil Cumbres

Angangueo

La Mesa

Chivati-Huacal

Lomas de Aparicio

Zitácuaro

Cerro Pelon

San F. Oxtotilpan

Piedra Herrado

Palomas

Gulf of Mexico

Mexico City

Toluca

MEXICO

PACIFIC OCEAN

MEXICO

N

Monarch butterfly colony
★ Capital
• City
□ Town

(Mexican location detail)

The eastern monarchs migrate to just twelve mountaintops, all located in central Mexico.

Trees that appear orange are covered with butterflies and roughly mark the border of this colony.

Many scientists were worried. The population of eastern monarchs had dropped more than 90 percent in just seventeen years.

At the same time, scientists in California reported that the number of western monarchs was dropping as well. From 1997 to 2014, the number of monarchs overwintering along the California coast had fallen by 74 percent.

Populations of overwintering monarchs were falling fast. By 2014 their numbers had fallen so far that people wondered whether the monarch butterfly should be listed as an endangered species—a species in danger of becoming extinct, or disappearing forever.

Losing monarchs could be bad for our world because monarchs play an important part in the food web. Despite the milkweed toxins in their bodies, they are food for songbirds, spiders, and insects. Monarchs visit many flowers and act as pollinators. Among pollinating insects, monarchs are very well studied and may be telling us something big is going wrong with our environment. If monarchs are in trouble, that could be a sign that other insect pollinators—not to mention other migrating animals—could be in trouble too.

Losing monarchs would be terrible for people too. Monarchs are the official state insect of seven US states and a familiar summertime sight across the United States and Canada. Many students raise monarchs in their classrooms and learn about their life cycle. In both California and Mexico, people celebrate the return of the monarchs every year. Without monarchs, people would lose a favorite insect and a way to connect to the natural world.

Scientists had a new mystery to solve. What was happening to the monarchs?

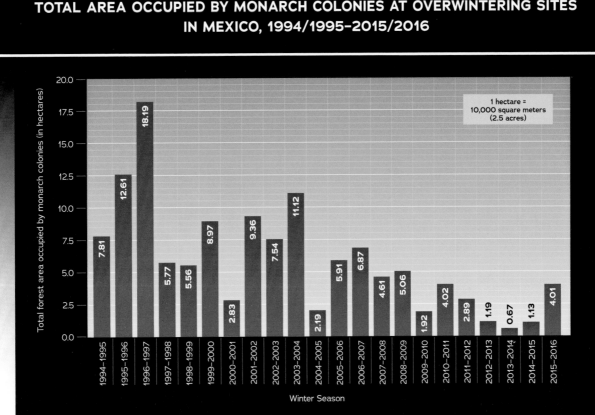

TOTAL AREA OCCUPIED BY MONARCH COLONIES AT OVERWINTERING SITES IN MEXICO, 1994/1995–2015/2016

1 hectare =
10,000 square meters
(2.5 acres)

Total forest area occupied by monarch colonies (in hectares)

Winter Season

Winter Season	Value
1994–1995	7.81
1995–1996	12.61
1996–1997	18.19
1997–1998	5.77
1998–1999	5.56
1999–2000	8.97
2000–2001	2.83
2001–2002	9.36
2002–2003	7.54
2003–2004	11.12
2004–2005	2.19
2005–2006	5.91
2006–2007	6.87
2007–2008	4.61
2008–2009	5.06
2009–2010	1.92
2010–2011	4.02
2011–2012	2.89
2012–2013	1.19
2013–2014	0.67
2014–2015	1.13
2015–2016	4.01

The total area of the winter colonies has fallen between 1994–1995 and 2015–2016, and it hit an all-time low in the winter of 2013–2014.

The monarchs that make it to Mexico are true survivors. Many monarchs lose their lives before they can complete the journey.

CHAPTER 2
Monarchs in Trouble

Something was causing the winter colonies of monarchs in Mexico to shrink. But what was it? Scientists realized that a change must be happening somewhere in some part of the monarch's yearly cycle. They would have to look at what was going on in all the different places that monarchs live and travel throughout the year—in the winter forests, across the summer breeding grounds, and along the spring and fall migration routes. Scientists would have to study any changes they found and try to understand how those could be affecting the monarch population.

THE WINTER FORESTS ARE GROWING DEADLIER

Biologist Lincoln Brower has been visiting the Mexican monarch colonies since soon after their discovery in the late 1970s. He says the winter forests have changed and become more dangerous for monarchs. Historically, oyamel forests have had the exact conditions that monarchs need to survive the winter. The temperature in the winter forest usually stays between 32°F and 55°F (0°C and 13°C). Any colder and the monarchs would freeze. Any warmer and they would burn up their stored fat too quickly. The trees protect the monarchs from bad weather and storms, from cold, wind, rain, and snow. "The trees are a blanket that keeps them warm," said Brower. "They are an umbrella that keeps them from getting wet." The forests form their own small climate—a microclimate—that is different from the surrounding climate.

The challenge for Brower and others who want to protect the butterflies is that oyamel trees are valuable not only to monarchs but also to people. Many people live near the monarch colonies. They cut down trees from the forest and use the wood to build homes and tools and to cook their food, and some people sell the wood to make money.

A man cuts down a tree in the monarch butterfly sanctuary near Ocampo, Mexico. Damage to the winter sanctuaries puts the butterflies at risk from rainfall and winter storms.

Cutting down trees can harm the monarchs in two ways. If all the trees in a monarch sanctuary are cut down—a type of logging known as clear-cutting—then the monarchs lose a winter home. But the removal of even a small number of trees from the forest can also harm the monarchs. Cutting down a few trees here and there weakens the protective microclimate. It creates openings in the forest canopy (the leafy upper branches of the trees). These openings let in dangerous cold, wind, rain, and snow.

Winter storms have been bringing rain and snow to the monarch colonies for a long time. But with logging of the forest, the toll of these storms has grown worse. In some years, winter storms kill huge numbers of overwintering monarchs. In 2002, for example, a severe storm killed as many as five hundred million monarchs. With each deadly storm, fewer survivors are able to begin the journey north in spring. The losses from a winter storm can ripple through the monarch's entire yearly cycle, resulting in smaller colonies the next year.

A DRY SPRING SPELLS DANGER

Scientist Elise Zipkin wondered how climate could be affecting monarchs. Climate is the average weather in a particular place over a long time. Scientists know Earth's climate is changing. Average temperatures are rising, and patterns of rainfall are shifting. Zipkin wondered what effects these changes in climate were having on monarchs.

The question is a complicated one, because climate can affect both the monarchs and the food they eat. Weather that is too hot—or too cold—can kill caterpillars and butterflies. Weather that is too hot and dry can shrivel milkweed and nectar plants. To make things even more complicated, monarchs encounter different climates throughout their yearly cycle. A change in the climate during one part of their journey could lead to a drop in the population somewhere else.

To investigate the effects of climate, Zipkin and her team studied butterfly counts made by citizen scientists in two states, Ohio and Illinois. At numerous locations across each state, citizen scientists had carried out weekly surveys in which they counted and identified all the butterflies they saw, including monarchs. From these surveys, Zipkin's team could estimate how many summer monarchs were living at different places in Ohio and Illinois each year from 1996 to 2011.

Next, the scientists studied weather patterns at different places where monarchs live and travel. Could they find a link between the size of the summer population in those two states and the weather in some place during part of the monarch's yearly cycle?

Yes, said Zipkin. The place that stood out was Texas. "What's going on in the spring in Texas can have a big effect," said Zipkin.

But why would Texas matter? The reason is that all the eastern migrating monarchs travel through Texas in the spring. Texas is where many surviving females (the ones that spent winter in Mexico) lay their eggs. And Texas is where those offspring hatch, turn into butterflies, and continue the journey north. So the spring weather in Texas can influence the size of the summer population.

The Texas effect is so big that scientists can look at early spring conditions there and

Elise Zipkin discovered that spring weather in Texas has a big effect on the number of summer monarchs.

Monarchs fuel up on nectar at a Texas garden. The eastern monarchs funnel through Texas every spring and fall.

predict how many summer monarchs there will be farther north. Summer monarchs are most plentiful when Texas has a cool, rainy spring.

Zipkin's finding could partly explain the shrinking colonies in Mexico. From 2010 to 2015, Texas experienced a record-breaking drought—a severe dry spell. Little rain fell across the state. Flowers and milkweed shriveled. Streams and pools where butterflies could drink dried up. During those same years, the Mexico population hit record lows.

The drought has ended, but scientists predict that severe droughts could become more common in Texas. This could present ongoing problems for monarchs and make it difficult for the overwintering population to return to a healthy size.

If climate in Texas is important for the spring monarchs, maybe it's important for the fall butterflies too. Fall monarchs pass through Texas on their journey south to Mexico. How does climate affect the number of monarchs that survive the fall migration? This is a question scientists would also like to understand.

MILKWEED IS DISAPPEARING

Scientists say overwintering monarchs could be disappearing because of a change in summer habitat. In spring and summer, monarchs lay their eggs on milkweed, but the places where milkweed grows have changed. In some areas, people have built towns and cities where fields of milkweed once grew. Homes, streets, schools, shopping centers, and office buildings have replaced it.

Farms have changed too. Milkweed once sprouted among rows of crop plants. According to monarch scientist Karen Oberhauser, milkweed that grew in farm fields made an excellent habitat for monarchs. In 2000 she and other scientists walked through cornfields in multiple Midwestern states and counted all the eggs and caterpillars they could find. They found a lot. "There were monarchs using that milkweed," Oberhauser said. "They were surviving on it really well." The scientists calculated that farm fields were an important part of monarch habitat in Midwestern farming states such as Kansas, Nebraska, Iowa, Missouri, Wisconsin, Illinois, Michigan, Indiana, and Ohio. This is a region known as the Corn Belt.

But farm fields have changed since Oberhauser and her colleagues did their study, and farm milkweed has mostly disappeared from the Corn Belt. In the 1990s, many farmers began to use a new way of growing corn and soybeans. They planted seeds that were genetically modified, meaning scientists had changed the seeds' genes in a deliberate way. These new plants had been designed to resist herbicide, a chemical that kills plants.

Farmers spray herbicide to kill weeds, which would otherwise crowd out their crops and rob their crop plants of water and nutrients. Traditionally, a farmer who wanted to use herbicide had to spray it early in the spring, before the crops were growing. If the herbicide was sprayed too late, it would kill the crop plants along with the weeds. These early spring sprayings meant that milkweed escaped harm because it emerges from the ground later in the year.

But with the new herbicide-resistant seeds, a farmer could spray herbicide later in the year without harming the crops. The new seeds meant that the weeds would die, but the corn and soybean would grow fine. Many farmers loved the new crops because they could spray herbicide after their crops were growing, which gave them a way to grow corn and soybean with fewer weeds.

A sprayer applies herbicide to a field of corn in Illinois.

But scientists suspected that the increased spraying of herbicide was harming milkweed. Oberhauser teamed up with biologist John Pleasants to study what was happening. From 2000 to 2008, they measured patches of milkweed in farm fields where farmers were growing the new herbicide-resistant corn and soybean plants. Those farmers were spraying more herbicide and spraying it when milkweed was growing. Year by year, the scientists watched what happened to the patches of milkweed. "All these patches were shrinking," Pleasants said. Finally, the milkweed disappeared altogether.

Pleasants calculated that between 1999 and 2014, 850 million milkweed plants disappeared from corn and soybean fields. As milkweed vanished, female monarchs lost places to lay their eggs. Females in the Corn Belt had to spend more time searching for milkweed and had to fly farther to find it, and as a result, they laid fewer eggs each summer. Many scientists think the loss of milkweed in the Corn Belt is a big reason why the monarch colonies in Mexico have shrunk.

THE WRONG MILKWEED INTERRUPTS THE MIGRATION

Could the colonies be shrinking because monarchs are no longer migrating to Mexico? In the early 2000s, monarch scientist Sonia Altizer began getting calls from people who lived across the southern United States, from North Carolina to Texas. The callers reported seeing monarchs in their gardens in December, January, and February. Instead of migrating, the butterflies were staying put for the winter. Some of the butterflies had crumpled wings.

Altizer's team investigated to find out what was going on. At every place, they found the monarchs were feeding during the winter on a plant called tropical milkweed (*Asclepias curassavica*).

Tropical milkweed grows naturally in Mexico, the Caribbean, and Central America. It grows in the United States and Canada only when people buy it at garden centers and plant it in their yards and gardens. Tropical milkweed grows in a different way than native species of milkweed, the ones that normally grow in the United States and Canada. Native milkweeds go dormant in winter. They drop their leaves, survive as roots underground, and begin sprouting new shoots again in the spring. But tropical milkweed is different. In places where winters are mild, it can keep making flowers and growing new leaves all winter long.

In response to this new source of winter milkweed, monarchs began to skip the trip to Mexico. They stuck around and continued breeding all winter long. Skipping the migration and breeding in winter may not seem like a problem. But remember the crumpled wings people saw? Those can be a symptom of a disease known as OE (short for *Ophryocystis elektroscirrha*).

OE is a type of protozoan that infects monarch butterflies, coating the outside of their bodies with tiny, seedlike spores. Infected monarchs spread the disease to other monarchs.

Tropical milkweed (*Asclepias curassavica*) (*top*) is not native to the United States and Canada. It is easily recognized by its red and orange flowers. Common milkweed (*Asclepias syriaca*) (*bottom*) is a species that is native to southern Canada and the eastern United States.

This monarch is heavily infected with the OE parasite and is stuck emerging from its chrysalis.

Here's how: The spores fall off infected butterflies onto milkweed leaves, and caterpillars ingest the spores as they are eating the leaves. OE grows and multiplies within the caterpillar and then the chrysalis. Adult butterflies climb out of their chrysalises covered with spores, and the cycle continues. A monarch with severe OE may be so weak that it gets stuck inside its chrysalis skin and dies. Or it may emerge but have crumpled wings, which prevents it from flying. In mild cases, an infected monarch looks fine, but it won't live as long or fly as well as a healthy monarch.

Scientist Dara Satterfield says OE has probably been infecting monarchs for a long time. But migration keeps the rate of infection low. A butterfly with mild OE is a weak flier and may die before it arrives in Mexico. That's a good thing. "By the end of the journey, the population is actually healthier," said Satterfield.

But if the act of migrating keeps OE infection rates low, could skipping the migration put monarchs at greater risk for OE? Scientists investigated. With the help of over a hundred citizen scientists, they caught monarchs across the eastern United States and Canada. They caught them in places where they migrate, in places where they were breeding in winter, and at the oyamel forests in Mexico. Then they tested each monarch for OE by gently pressing a piece of clear tape against the butterfly's abdomen. Citizen scientists mailed the tape to scientists, who counted spores under a microscope.

What they discovered is that monarchs that had stopped migrating were far more likely to be infected with OE. About 50 percent of those monarchs were infected with OE. And in some places with tropical milkweed, 100 percent of winter-breeding monarchs had the disease. In contrast, only about 10 percent of migrating monarchs had OE infections.

Breeding in winter appears to be bad for butterflies because it allows OE infection to build up, weakening the population. Scientists don't yet know if the nonmigrating butterflies can spread OE to migrating butterflies. If they do spread the disease, this could cause infection rates to go up throughout the population. It might lead to fewer butterflies completing the journey to Mexico.

THE PUZZLING FALL MIGRATION

Could there be other things killing monarchs? Many scientists think so. Some point to the fall migration, which they think has grown deadlier in recent years. But nobody knows for sure if this is true. Elise Zipkin said, "We know less about the fall migration than we [know about] other times of the year."

What might be harming monarchs on the journey south? One possible suspect is the loss of wildflowers. During the fall, monarchs must gorge on nectar as they fly south across thousands of miles. They visit fall flowers like asters, blazing star, and goldenrod. Monarchs drink so much nectar that they actually gain weight on their journey.

"By the time they get to Mexico, they're butterballs. They use that fat to get them through the winter and back to Texas," explained Lincoln Brower. But wildflowers, along with milkweed, have been disappearing from many places. As people have built cities and towns—and as farmers have sprayed more herbicide—wildflowers have become harder to find. Without enough nectar along their route, the monarchs may not have enough fuel to make it to Mexico.

Another suspect is cars. Migrating monarchs are at risk of colliding with cars when they cross roads. Scientists have studied this problem by collecting dead butterflies along roadways in Canada, the United States, and Mexico. They have concluded that large numbers of monarchs die in car collisions throughout the spring and summer, and the number rises even higher during the fall migration. Yet nobody knows just how big a bite this is taking out of the monarch population or whether the problem is growing worse. Scientists must do more research to better understand how car collisions are affecting how many monarchs make it to Mexico.

A third suspect is pesticides, chemicals that are used to kill pests, particularly insects. People use pesticides on farms and around homes, schools, and other buildings. Some newer pesticides

Collisions with cars kill a high number of monarchs every year.

called neonicotinoids—or neonics (NEE-oh-nics) for short—are similar to the natural chemical nicotine. Neonics act on an insect's nervous system, blocking nerve pathways and paralyzing the insect. When neonics are sprayed on plants or injected into the soil, the plant absorbs them through their roots or leaves. The chemicals move throughout the whole plant, so that all parts of the plant become toxic to insects. Then, when a caterpillar takes a bite of a leaf, it gets a dose of pesticide.

Neonics can remain in the environment for months or years, and during this time, they can spread to new plants. Pesticide spray or dust can drift in the wind or wash into the groundwater, moving to nearby plants and harming the insects that eat those plants.

Neonics first became available in the mid-1990s, and since then they've become the most widely used pesticides in the world. Could neonics be harming monarchs? Researchers tested the effects of these pesticides in the laboratory by feeding caterpillars milkweed leaves that contain these chemicals. High doses of pesticide killed the caterpillars. With low doses, the caterpillars survived but were smaller than normal.

It's difficult to know what dose of these chemicals monarchs might be exposed to in the wild. Because neonics act on an insect's nervous system, scientists think the chemicals could interfere with the ability of adult monarchs to migrate. Scientists will need to carry out more research to discover whether neonics are harming monarchs in the wild and what effect they could be having on the number of migrating monarchs that reach Mexico.

Monarchs depend on milkweed as the sole food of their caterpillars. The fate of the insect is closely linked to the availability of milkweed.

CHAPTER 3
Bringing the Monarchs Back

Scientists have identified a whole lot of changes that could be harming the eastern monarchs, and these changes could be adding up. Although the western monarchs are not as well studied, scientists say they could be getting hit with similar changes. Elise Zipkin said, "All these little things are really contributing to the loss of monarchs at every step of this annual cycle."

Yet nobody knows how much each individual change contributes to the decline of the whole population. Researchers continue to sift through data, much of it collected by citizen scientists, to understand how the cycle is breaking down so they can fix the problem. At the same time, scientists, citizen scientists, and butterfly lovers are joining forces to help bring the monarchs back.

TWO HOPEFUL THINGS ABOUT MONARCHS

One hopeful thing about monarchs is that they have the ability to bounce back with big numbers. Given the right conditions, each female can lay hundreds of eggs. So if circumstances improve, the monarch population could return to a healthy size quickly.

Gardeners can be good friends to butterflies. People can give monarchs a helping hand by encouraging wildflowers to grow in their community.

Here's another hopeful thing about monarchs: individual people can make a difference. If you want to help, here are a few things you can do:

- Create a monarch habitat. If you live in the continental United States or southern Canada, you can plant a habitat for monarchs in your own yard, at your school, or at a local nature center. Choose native milkweeds for caterpillars. Include nectar flowers for butterflies, especially flowers that bloom during the fall migration.

- Protect your garden from pesticides. When you buy plants for your yard, school, or nature center, ask the garden center staff if the plants were treated with neonics (or with any of these pesticides, which include neonics: Acetamiprid, Clothianidin, Dinotefuran, Imidacloprid, Thiacloprid, or Thiamethoxam). If the answer is yes, don't buy those plants! Instead, find organically grown plants, which are never treated with neonics.

- Get involved in citizen science. Scientists rely on citizen scientists to help them understand all stages of the monarch's annual cycle. For more about specific groups you can get involved with, check out the "Become a Citizen Scientist" list near the end of this book.
- Spread the word. Talk with your family, friends, and neighbors. Educate people you know about monarchs, and explain how everyone can help.

THE SEARCH FOR ANSWERS

Without a doubt, monarchs are facing a lot of new dangers. But which ones are the big ones, the dangers that are taking the biggest bite out of the monarch population? Scientists do not agree on the answer. Some think the biggest problem is lack of milkweed. Their hypothesis is that shrinking summer habitat in the Corn Belt is a main reason the population in Mexico has fallen. But some scientists disagree. Although they agree that milkweed has disappeared from many farms, they think there is still plenty of milkweed in other places. Their hypothesis is that something big is going wrong during the fall migration, and that monarchs are leaving in the fall but not reaching Mexico.

It is normal for scientists to have different hypotheses. As they continue to test each hypothesis and search for answers, they may come to agree on an accepted theory of what changes are most harmful. If they do, they will better understand how to help make the world a safer place for monarchs.

Elise Zipkin is continuing her search for answers, looking for clues in data collected by citizen scientists. In some places, people have carried out butterfly surveys for many years. Zipkin and her team are using these surveys to zero in on particular places, like a meadow or a park, and find out whether there are fewer monarchs there than in the past. Then they can examine what else about that place has changed.

Has the amount of nearby milkweed dropped? What were weather conditions like? As they look at place after place, Zipkin hopes that patterns will emerge. Those patterns may reveal what changes are most important to monarchs. "It's like detective work. We're trying to figure out what's going on," Zipkin said.

PROTECT THE WINTER FORESTS

Ever since the discovery of the overwintering sites, scientists and conservationists have stressed how important it is to protect the oyamel forests. In 1986 the Mexican government created the Monarch Butterfly Biosphere Special Reserve. In 2000 the government expanded the reserve and added more protections for the monarch colonies.

Within each monarch sanctuary, logging is forbidden in a central core zone. In a surrounding buffer zone, a small amount of logging is allowed. People who own land in the core zone are paid money each year *not* to cut down the forest. The Mexican government and local communities work to protect the forests.

The good news is that large-scale illegal logging within the monarch sanctuaries has mostly stopped. Unfortunately, small-scale logging continues to be a problem. Local people still sometimes cut down trees for fuel and building materials. Better enforcement is needed. Guards and local residents must work together to patrol the forests, prevent logging, and keep the forests intact and safe for monarchs.

Both the monarchs and the people living near the monarchs are important. So how can the needs of both be met? One solution has been tourism. At some sanctuaries, tourists come to see the butterflies, and this gives villagers a way to earn money. Villagers sell souvenirs, cook food for tourists, provide horseback rides, and serve as tour guides to the sanctuaries. Yet tourism carries risks as well—too many tourists can damage the forests and harm monarchs. Scientists and others who care about the monarchs continue to look for solutions that will meet the needs of the people and the butterflies.

Can this monarch sanctuary in Mexico be preserved? The answer will be decided by future actions that people take.

CREATE A MILKWEED CORRIDOR

Starting in about 2013, as word traveled that monarchs were in trouble, people in North America became concerned. Many people began planting butterfly gardens. Even a tiny patch of unused ground can become monarch habitat. All it takes is native milkweed for caterpillars and nectar flowers for adult butterflies. After one person plants a butterfly garden, neighbors may be inspired to do the same, and as more and more people plant a patch of habitat, the patches become a corridor. The corridor becomes both a breeding place and a passageway to help monarchs make it back to their winter home.

Planting butterfly gardens is only the beginning. Scientists and conservation groups have set a goal to add over one billion milkweed plants back to the landscape. They are looking to restore habitat in all sorts of places, with plantings in backyards, schoolyards, and parks; in fields and ditches; along railroads and power lines; and beside roads.

But aren't roads dangerous places for monarchs? After all, large numbers of them get hit by cars every year. What's more, roadsides can contain high amounts of harmful chemicals, like road salts and heavy metals. With these problems, why try to restore monarch habitat along roads?

Scientist Holly Holt says while it is true that roads can be dangerous, it is important

Roadside milkweed, like these plants growing in Iowa, can help replace milkweed that has disappeared from farms.

to consider that not all roads are equally bad for monarchs. A country road with little traffic may be a safer place for habitat restoration than a busy highway. Besides, says Holt, the loss of milkweed in other places makes roadsides especially important. "That habitat along roadsides may become more valuable just because there are fewer milkweeds around."

The benefits of creating habitat corridors go beyond butterflies. The numbers of bees, birds, and other pollinator species are going down. Restoring diverse habitat, with milkweed and a range of nectar plants, will help many other species too.

GO NATIVE

Initially, when the news got out about monarchs and the loss of milkweed, many people who wanted to help bought milkweed at local garden centers. But the milkweed most often sold at garden stores is tropical milkweed. Scientists did not discover until

2015 that tropical milkweed encourages monarchs to breed in winter, with bad results. "It's important that we address [the problem of tropical milkweed] now so that it doesn't become even more of a problem," said Dara Satterfield.

So scientists began spreading the word that native milkweeds are healthier for monarchs. In response, gardeners began to seek out native milkweeds instead. Garden centers have also started to respond, and native milkweeds are becoming more available.

But what about people who already have tropical milkweed growing in their yard? Scientists say the best option is to dig it up and throw it away, but if that's not possible, people can chop it down to within 6 inches (15 cm) of the ground and keep chopping it down from October to February. That way, monarchs will flutter on by and keep going to Mexico. But eventually, Satterfield said, the goal is for people to remove tropical milkweeds and plant native milkweeds in their place.

Monarchs fuel up on nectar at purple coneflowers. Fall wildflowers provide essential nourishment for monarchs heading south.

A tree covered with wintering monarchs. As more people join the effort to help, can monarch populations come back?

CONCLUSION
Butterflies on the Brink

Every December researchers with the World Wildlife Fund Mexico and the Monarch Butterfly Biosphere Special Reserve head into the oyamel forests to measure the colonies. And every year, monarch scientists and monarch lovers across North America wait to hear the news. The results, announced in late winter, are like a report card for how the population is doing.

So how is the population doing? By the winter of 2015–2016, the monarch population seemed to be fluttering back. The colonies that year covered 10 acres (4 ha), up from a very low 1.7 acres (0.7 ha) in 2014. But the following year, the population fell again, to 7.2 acres (2.9 ha).

Why did the colonies grow only to shrink again? Scientists think the population may have grown in 2015–2016 because the drought in Texas ended. But as that winter was ending, a severe storm struck the colonies just as the monarchs were beginning to head north. That storm may have been the reason the colonies were smaller again the following winter.

A guide (*left*) leads a tour group through the Sierra Chincua butterfly sanctuary.

Scientists would like to see the colonies cover at least 14.8 acres (6 ha) from year to year. This is the size that is needed, they say, for the monarch population to be out of danger.

For now, monarch butterflies still fly in fields of flowers. They still carry out their amazing migration from across the United States and Canada, flying thousands of miles to the mountains of central Mexico. But the world has become a dangerous place for monarchs. Scientists, citizen scientists, and other butterfly lovers continue to work together to keep the monarchs and their migration from disappearing forever. The challenge they face is to increase the size of the winter colonies. They are driven by the dream of a future where monarchs continue to fill the skies. But for now, the future for monarchs remains uncertain.

AUTHOR'S NOTE

The scientific study of monarch butterflies has always been full of mystery. The original mystery—where do monarchs spend the winter?—has been replaced by a new one: Why are fewer monarchs returning to Mexico than in the past?

It was a joy to talk with scientists, citizen scientists, and monarch lovers. I would like to thank the following people for sharing their knowledge and perspectives with me: Anurag Agruwal, Cornell University; Lincoln Brower, Sweet Briar College; Wendy Caldwell, Monarch Joint Venture; Andy Davis, University of Georgia; Pam and Doug Ford, Snetsinger Butterfly Garden; Holly Holt, Monarch Joint Venture; Elise Zipkin, Michigan State University; John Pleasants, Iowa State University; Karen Oberhauser, University of Minnesota; Dara Satterfield, Smithsonian National Zoo; Gayle Steffy; and Justin Wheeler, Xerces Society.

I would also like to thank Todd Biddle and his hardworking horticulture students at Bald Eagle High School; Stacy Shaw and all the monarch-loving students, teachers, and staff at West Branch School; and the fifth-grade butterfly gardeners at Corl Street Elementary. And finally, a big thank-you to Ellie Hirsch, Eva Hirsch, and Joe Peters for venturing into an overgrown field to catch and tag monarchs with me.

Here in Pennsylvania, 2016 was a good year for monarchs. I saw many caterpillars and butterflies in fields and in my backyard while researching and writing this book. But overall, monarchs are struggling. We may never again see the numbers of monarchs that existed when I was growing up. But if we all work together, perhaps we can ensure that in the future, children will still have a chance to experience the thrill of holding a monarch in their hands and watching it lift off on its amazing migration.

GLOSSARY

abdomen: the hind part of an insect's body

breeding ground: the place where an animal mates and completes its life cycle. The monarch butterfly breeding grounds occur across North America wherever milkweed grows.

caterpillar: the larval stage of the butterfly life cycle

chrysalis: the pupal stage of the butterfly life cycle

citizen scientist: a nonscientist who studies the natural world and collects data to send to scientists

colony: a population of animals of the same type that live together. Monarch butterflies gather in winter colonies in Mexico by the millions.

dormant: not growing or carrying out biological activity. In cold climates, many plants go dormant during the winter.

drought: a long period of dry weather

egg: the first stage of the butterfly life cycle

genetically modified: a plant or animal species in which the genetic material has been altered in order to change one or more of its characteristics

herbicide: a chemical substance used to kill plants

herbicide-resistant: capable of resisting a herbicide. Plants that are herbicide-resistant can continue to grow when treated with a herbicide.

milkweed: a group of North American plants with milky juice and clusters of flowers. Milkweed is the monarch butterfly's host plant, the plant upon which it lays its eggs.

monarch sanctuary: a place where monarch butterflies gather for the winter

native: living or growing naturally in a particular place

nectar: the sweet liquid produced by flowers

neonicotinoid pesticide: a kind of insect-killing chemical that is similar to nicotine. Nicotine occurs naturally in tobacco plants. Neonicotinoid pesticides are often referred to as *neonics*.

***Ophryocystis elektroscirrha* (OE):** a protozoan that weakens or kills monarch butterflies

overwinter: to survive through the winter

oyamel: a species of fir tree (*Abies religiosa*) that grows in the mountains of central Mexico. Monarch butterflies spend the winter clustered on oyamel trees.

pesticide: a chemical substance used to kill insects or other living things that are considered to be pests

pollinator: an insect or other animal that pollinates flowers, helping them make seeds

proboscis: a tubelike mouthpart that butterflies use to drink nectar from flowers

survey: a study that collects data about a group of living things, such as butterflies, living in a particular place

tropical milkweed: a species of milkweed (*Asclepias curassavica*) that occurs naturally in Mexico and Central America

FURTHER READING

Burns, Loree Griffin. *Citizen Scientists*. New York: Henry Holt, 2012.
This book looks at young citizen scientists involved in projects to study monarch butterflies, birds, frogs, and ladybugs.

Burris, Judy, and Wayne Richards. *The Life Cycles of Butterflies: From Egg to Maturity, a Visual Guide to 23 Common Garden Butterflies*. North Adams, MA: Storey Pub., 2006.
Get an up-close look at a variety of butterfly species. This book showcases the egg, caterpillar, chrysalis, and emerging butterfly, giving readers a chance to compare and contrast at each stage.

Pasternak, Carol. *How to Raise Monarch Butterflies: A Step-by-Step Guide for Kids.* Buffalo: Firefly Books, 2012.
A great way to get to know monarchs is to observe their life cycle from caterpillar to chrysalis to adult. This book gives you detailed instructions on how to raise monarch butterflies from caterpillars you find. You can raise monarchs if you live in the continental United States, in Hawaii, or in southern Canada.

BECOME A CITIZEN SCIENTIST

An exciting way to help monarchs is to become a citizen scientist. You and your family can choose from a wide range of options, depending on what activities interest you. On some of the websites listed, you can check in and read regular updates of how the monarchs are doing.

Journey North
http://www.journeynorth.org/monarch
Each fall and spring, students and scientists track the monarch migration. If you live in the continental United States, you can observe and report your first monarch sighting of the year, the first spring milkweed to emerge, whether there are monarchs in winter in your area, and more. Your reports, along with those of other citizen scientists, are made into interactive maps that allow you to watch the migration unfold. Journey North also has regular news reports (available at http://www.learner.org/jnorth/monarch/News.html) that highlight how this year's migration is unfolding.

Monarch Health
http://www.monarchparasites.org
If you'd like to help track the spread of OE, this website will get you started. Participants in the continental United States can capture or raise wild monarchs, press tape against the monarch's body to collect parasite spores, and send your sample to monarch scientists. You'll find information on how to order free sampling kits on the website.

Monarch Larva Monitoring Project
http://monarchlab.org/mlmp
This project is helping monarch scientists study monarch populations during the breeding season. Volunteers throughout the continental United States do weekly surveys of monarch eggs and caterpillars, measure changes in milkweed plants, observe monarch parasites, and more. With many different activities, you can choose to do as many or as few of the activities as you like.

Monarch Watch
http://www.monarchwatch.org
This is the tagging program that tracks eastern monarchs during their fall migration. Recovered tags help answer questions about the pace and timing of the migration and which butterflies are most likely to make it to Mexico. To date, more than 1.2 million monarchs have been tagged and over 16,000 have been recovered. You can participate if you live east of the Rocky Mountains. You can order tagging kits with numbered tags and instructions on the website. You'll find updates on how well the monarchs are doing on the Monarch Watch blog (monarchwatch.org/blog/).

Western Monarch Thanksgiving Count
http://www.westernmonarchcount.org/
Every year volunteers in California collect data on the population of western monarchs wintering along the California coast. Volunteers visit the same overwintering sites year after year and count monarchs over the Thanksgiving holiday.

PLANT A BUTTERFLY GARDEN

Another fun way to get involved with monarchs is to plant a butterfly garden. These resources will help you along the way.

Milkweed Seed Finder
http://www.xerces.org/milkweed-seed-finder/
Use the milkweed seed finder to locate milkweed seeds that are native to your area. Also check out the lists of nectar plants for different parts of the country (http://www.xerces.org/monarch-nectar -plants/). Click on the map to find a list of native plants for monarchs that grow where you live.

Monarch Joint Venture Success Stories
http://monarchjointventure.org/success-stories/map-of-successes/
Get inspired by what other people around the country are doing to create habitat for monarchs. You can see photos, read what people are planting, and learn how they are caring for their habitat. Then you can add your own butterfly habitat to the map. Your habitat will become part of the Million Pollinator Garden Challenge, a nationwide effort to create gardens that help butterflies, bees, and other pollinators.

Monarch Watch's Monarch Waystation Program
http://monarchwatch.org/waystations/index.html
Once you've created a monarch habitat, you can certify your habitat as a Monarch Waystation, a place that provides the plants that monarchs need to sustain their migration. You'll pay a small fee and receive a Monarch Waystation sign you can post in your habitat.

SOURCE NOTES

10 Homero Aridjis, "Last Call for Monarchs," *Huffington Post*, accessed August 30, 2017, http://www .huffingtonpost.com/homero-aridjis/mexico-monarch-butterfly-migration-_b_4745915.html.

11 Fred A. Urquhart, "Found at Last: The Monarch's Winter Home," *National Geographic*, August 1976, http://ngm.nationalgeographic.com/1976/08/monarch-butterflies/urquhart-text.

12 Monika Maeckle, "Founder of the Monarch Butterfly Roosting Sites in Mexico Lives a Quiet Life in Austin, Texas," July 10, 2012, http://texasbutterflyranch.com/2012/07/10/founder-of-the-monarch -butterfly-roosting-sites-in-mexico-lives-a-quiet-life-in-austin-texas/.

12 Urquhart, "Found at Last."

12 Fred A. Urquhart, *The Monarch Butterfly: International Traveler* (Chicago: Nelson-Hall, 1987), 158.

24 Lincoln Brower, telephone interview with author, December 7, 2016.

26 Elise Zipkin, telephone interview with author, November 17, 2016.

28 Karen Oberhauser, telephone interview with author, October 17, 2016.

30 John Pleasants, telephone interview with author, November 17, 2016.

32 Dara Satterfield, telephone interview with author, November 22, 2016.

33 Zipkin, telephone interview.

34 Joel Achenbach. "Monarch Butterflies Face Tough Trip through Texas," *Washington Post*, October 7, 2011, https://www.washingtonpost.com/national/health-science/can-monarch-butterflies-make-it -through-texas/2011/10/07/gIQAEt8ySL_story.html?utm_term=.75dd0bab97c3.

37 Zipkin, telephone interview.

40 Ibid.

42 Wendy Caldwell and Holly Holt, telephone interview with author, September 15, 2016.

43 Satterfield, telephone interview.

SELECTED BIBLIOGRAPHY

Center for Biological Diversity and Center for Food Safety, the Xerces Society, and Lincoln Brower. "Petition to Protect the Monarch Butterfly (*Danaus Plexippus Plexippus*) under the Endangered Species Act." biologicaldiversity.org, August 26, 2014, https://www.biologicaldiversity.org/species /invertebrates/pdfs/Monarch_ESA_Petition.pdf.

Grace, Eric S. *The World of the Monarch Butterfly*. San Francisco: Sierra Club Books, 1997.

Oberhauser, Karen Suzanne, Kelly R. Nail, and Sonia M. Altizer, eds. *Monarchs in a Changing World: Biology and Conservation of an Iconic Butterfly*. Ithaca, NY: Comstock, 2015.

Pleasants, John, and Karen Oberhauser. "Milkweed Loss in Agricultural Fields Because of Herbicide Use: Effect on the Monarch Butterfly Population." *Insect Conservation and Diversity* (2012): 1–10.

Urquhart, Fred A. *The Monarch Butterfly: International Traveler*. Chicago: Nelson-Hall, 1987.

Zipkin, Elise F., Leslie Ries, Rick Reeves, James Regetz, and Karen S. Oberhauser. "Tracking Climate Impacts on the Migratory Monarch Butterfly." *Global Change Biology* 18 (2012): 3039–49.

INDEX

ABOUT THE AUTHOR

Rebecca E. Hirsch, PhD, is the award-winning author of numerous books about science, nature, and geography for children. A former plant biologist and molecular biologist, she lives with her husband and three children in State College, Pennsylvania. You can visit her online at www.rebeccahirsch.com.

PHOTO ACKNOWLEDGMENTS

The images in this book are used with the permission of: iStock.com/nelsonarts, p. 1; J Stromme/Alamy Stock Photo, pp. 2–3; age fotostock/Alamy Stock Photo, p. 4; © Captiva55/Shutterstock.com, p. 5; Courtesy of the author, p. 6 (all); © Pimmimemom/Dreamstime.com, pp. 6 (right), 7 (left); DUCLOS ALEXIS/SIPA/Newscom, p. 8; © Federal Newsphoto of Canada/Courtesy The University of Toronto Archives, p. 10; © Todd Strand/Independent Picture Service, p. 12; © Laura Westlund/Independent Picture Service, pp. 13, 16, 19, 21; Planetpix/Alamy Stock Photo, p. 14; iStock.com/rainbow-7, p. 15 (left); iStock.com/skhoward, p. 15 (right); age fotostock/Alamy Stock Photo, p. 17 (left); Jeff W. Jarrett/Shutterstock.com, p. 17 (right); © Photo by Lincoln Brower, Sweet Briar College, p. 20; Maya Moody/Alamy Stock Photo, p. 22; AP Photo/Gregory Bull, p. 24; Courtesy of Elise Zipkin, p. 26; Paul Wood/Alamy Stock Photo, p. 27; Design Pics Inc/Alamy Stock Photo, p. 29; Louise Heusinkveld/Alamy Stock Photo, p. 31 (top); iStock.com/helga_sm, p. 31 (bottom); © Jaap de Roode, p. 32; © Daniel Oines/flickr.com (CC BY 2.0), p. 34; Steve bly/Alamy Stock Photo, p. 36; iStock.com/kali9, p. 38; Richard Ellis/Alamy Stock Photo, p. 41; Nature and Science/Alamy Stock Photo, p. 42; Tracy Immordino/Alamy Stock Photo, p. 43; Tom Uhlman/Alamy Stock Photo, p. 44, Danita Delimont/Alamy Stock Photo, p. 46.

Front and back cover: © Captiva55/Shutterstock.com.

Spine: iStock.com/nelsonarts.